The

HOLY BIBLE

LEGACY STANDARD BIBLE

Containing the Gospel According to

JOHN

LEGACY STANDARD BIBLE

Gospel of John

Learn about our mission of distributing free Bibles. LegacyBibleFoundation.com.
Printed in China by codra.com ◊ 29 28 27 26 25 / 1 2 3 4 5. ALL RIGHTS RESERVED.

STEADFAST BIBLES is a division of THREE SIXTEEN PUBLISHING
Southern California

978-1-63664-380-9

God's Plan of Salvation

YOUR PROBLEM

Everyone is destined to die, but life does not end with death. The Bible says that after death there will be a judgment where each person will give an account of his or her life before God (Hebrews 4:13; 9:27). When we die, we will either live with God forever in Heaven or be separated from God in Hell.

Unfortunately, humanity's sinful nature and our ongoing choices to sin result in our living in disobedience to God: "for all have sinned and fall short of the glory of God" (Romans 3:23). This is humanity's problem: because of sin, every person is separated from God (Isaiah 59:2) and destined to spend eternity separated from Him.

People have tried to overcome this separation in many ways: by doing good, by practicing religion, by creating their own ideas of salvation, or by attempting to live a good moral life. However, none of these things is enough to cross the barrier of separation between God and humanity, because God is holy and human beings are sinful (Isaiah 64:6). Regardless of how good you think you are, every human has lied, stolen, hated, or otherwise disobeyed God's perfect will. We need to be saved from our sins and the judgment of God.

GOD'S LOVE

Yet, there is hope. Listen to the words of Jesus found in the very book you are holding in your hands:

> For God so loved the world, that He gave His only begotten Son, that whoever believes in Him shall not perish, but have eternal life. (John 3:16)

Although God has every right to condemn every person, because of His love He sent His Son, Jesus Christ. Jesus, the Son of God, was born as a man, lived a perfectly sinless life, and then was crucified. Since God is not a corrupt Judge, He does not simply sweep our sins under the rug—someone needs to be punished for them. Jesus sacrificed Himself to die on the cross to take the punishment of God that we deserve.

After Jesus Christ died on the cross, the Bible says that He rose from the dead! His resurrection life is a guarantee that Christians will also have eternal life. Eternal life not just about living forever, it's about having a loving relationship with God:

> And this is eternal life, that they may know You, the only true God, and Jesus Christ whom You have sent. (John 17:3)

WHAT NOW?

If you acknowledge that you are separated from God because you are a sinner who is in need of salvation, Scripture says you can receive God's gracious gift of eternal life—not by working for it—but by simply trusting in Jesus for salvation. Turn from your sins, and put your faith in Jesus as your Lord and Savior.

Begin attending a Christian church that preaches and teaches the Bible, share your newfound faith with others, and prayerfully read through the book you hold in your hands. The Apostle John lets us know why he wrote this book:

> but these have been written so that you may believe that Jesus is the Christ, the Son of God; and that believing you may have life in His name. (John 20:31)

May this narrative of the life of Jesus, as told by one of His closest friends, lead you to trust and believe in Him.

EXPLANATION OF TERMINOLOGY

The Bible is actually a collection of 66 books, originally written in Hebrew, Aramaic, and Greek. Since the Legacy Standard Bible (LSB) translation is committed to precisely representing what was written in the original languages, certain Greek terms used throughout the Gospel of John may differ slightly from how some modern English speakers understand those same terms.

The Terminology of Slave: The Greek term doulos, translated in the LSB as "slave", refers to an economic situation where someone was owned by another person. Unlike the transatlantic slave trade, ancient slavery was primarily a financial institution, was often entered into voluntarily (e.g., to pay off debt or to escape poverty), and was not normally motivated by racism. The Bible does not shy away from this term because it condemns all wicked forms of slavery (i.e., to sin, Satan, and death), highlights the power of redemption, and affirms that Christians were slaves of sin, but now are slaves belonging to the Lord Jesus Christ (Romans 6:16–22).

Gender Language: The LSB seeks to literally translate what was written in John's original Greek. The Greek language often used masculine words to describe both men and women, depending on the context. The word "man" can refer generically to "humanity", "he" can refer generically to a person "he/she", and so on.

Learn more about the Legacy Standard Bible translation at LSBible.org

EXPLANATION OF GENERAL FORMAT

Personal pronouns are capitalized when pertaining to Deity.

Italics are used in the text to indicate words which are not found in the original Greek but implied by it.

Small caps in the NT are used in the text to indicate OT quotations or obvious references to OT texts.

Asterisks are used to mark present tense verbs in Greek which have been translated with an English past tense in order to conform to modern usage (i.e., historical presents). The translators recognized that in some contexts the present tense seems more unexpected and unjustified to the English reader than a past tense would have been. For the sake of heightened vividness, Greek authors frequently used the present tense thereby transporting their readers in imagination to the actual scene at the time of occurrence. However, the translators felt that it would be wise to change these historical presents to English past tenses.

Brackets in text indicate words probably not in the original writings.

See "Foreword to the LSB" at LSBible.org
for more explanation of specific formatting styles.

The Gospel According to

JOHN

The Deity of Jesus Christ

1 In the beginning was the Word, and the Word
was with God, and the Word was God. 2 He was
in the beginning with God. 3 All things came into
being through Him, and apart from Him noth-
ing came into being that has come into being. 4 In
Him was life, and the life was the Light of men.
5 And the Light shines in the darkness, and the
darkness did not overtake it.

The Witness of John the Baptist

6 There was a man having been sent from God,
whose name was John. 7 He came as a witness,
to bear witness about the Light, so that all might
believe through him. 8 He was not the Light, but
he came to bear witness about the Light.

9 There was the true Light which, coming into
the world, enlightens everyone. 10 He was in the
world, and the world was made through Him, and
the world did not know Him. 11 He came to what
was His own, and those who were His own did
not receive Him. 12 But as many as received Him,
to them He gave the right to become children of
God, *even* to those who believe in His name, 13 who
were born, not of blood nor of the will of the flesh
nor of the will of man, but of God.

The Word Became Flesh

14 And the Word became flesh, and dwelt among
us, and we beheld His glory, glory as of the only
begotten from the Father, full of grace and truth.
15 John *bore witness about Him and cried out,
saying, "This was He of whom I said, 'He who
comes after me has been ahead of me, for He
existed before me.' " 16 For of His fullness we have
all received, and grace upon grace. 17 For the Law
was given through Moses; grace and truth came
through Jesus Christ. 18 No one has seen God at
any time; the only begotten God who is in the
bosom of the Father, He has explained *Him*.

A Voice in the Wilderness

19 And this is the witness of John, when the Jews
sent to him priests and Levites from Jerusalem
to ask him, "Who are you?" 20 And he confessed
and did not deny, but confessed, "I am not the
Christ." 21 And they asked him, "What then? Are
you Elijah?" And he *said, "I am not." "Are you the
Prophet?" And he answered, "No." 22 Therefore,
they said to him, "Who are you, so that we may
give an answer to those who sent us? What do you
say about yourself?" 23 He said, "I am A VOICE OF
ONE CRYING IN THE WILDERNESS, 'MAKE STRAIGHT
THE WAY OF THE LORD,' as Isaiah the prophet said."
24 Now they had been sent from the Pharisees.
25 And they asked him, and said to him, "Why then
are you baptizing, if you are not the Christ, nor
Elijah, nor the Prophet?" 26 John answered them,
saying, "I baptize with water, *but* among you
stands One whom you do not know. 27 *This One is*
He who comes after me, of whom I am not worthy
to untie the strap of His sandal." 28 These things
took place in Bethany beyond the Jordan, where
John was baptizing.

29 On the next day, he *saw Jesus coming to him

and *said, "Behold, the Lamb of God who takes
away the sin of the world! 30 This is He of whom I
said, 'After me comes a man who has been ahead
of me, for He existed before me.' 31 I did not know
Him, but so that He might be manifested to Israel,
I came baptizing with water." 32 And John bore wit-
ness saying, "I have beheld the Spirit descending
as a dove out of heaven, and He abided on Him.
33 And I did not know Him, but He who sent me
to baptize with water said to me, 'The One upon
whom you see the Spirit descending and abiding
on Him, this is the One who baptizes with the
Holy Spirit.' 34 And I myself have seen, and have
borne witness that this is the Son of God."

Behold, the Lamb of God

35 On the next day, John again was standing with
two of his disciples, 36 and he looked at Jesus as
He walked, and *said, "Behold, the Lamb of God!"
37 And the two disciples heard him speak and fol-
lowed Jesus. 38 And when Jesus turned and noticed
them following, He *said to them, "What do you
seek?" They said to Him, "Rabbi (which trans-
lated means Teacher), where are You staying?"

[39] He *said to them, “Come, and you will see.” So
they came and saw where He was staying; and
they stayed with Him that day. It was about the
tenth hour. [40] One of the two who heard John
speak and followed Him, was Andrew, Simon
Peter’s brother. [41] He first *found his own brother
Simon and *said to him, “We have found the
Messiah” (which translated means Christ). [42] He
brought him to Jesus. When Jesus looked at him,
He said, “You are Simon the son of John; you shall
be called Cephas” (which is translated Peter).

[43] On the next day, He desired to go into Galilee,
and He *found Philip. And Jesus *said to him,
“Follow Me.” [44] Now Philip was from Bethsaida,
the city of Andrew and Peter. [45] Philip *found
Nathanael and *said to him, “We have found Him
of whom Moses in the Law and *also* the Prophets
wrote—Jesus of Nazareth, the son of Joseph.”
[46] And Nathanael said to him, “Can any good
thing come out of Nazareth?” Philip *said to him,
“Come and see.” [47] Jesus saw Nathanael coming
to Him, and *said about him, “Behold, truly an
Israelite in whom there is no deceit!” [48] Nathanael
*said to Him, “From where do You know me?”

Jesus answered and said to him, "Before Philip
called you, when you were under the fig tree, I saw
you." 49 Nathanael answered Him, "Rabbi, You are
the Son of God; You are the King of Israel." 50 Jesus
answered and said to him, "Because I said to you
that I saw you under the fig tree, do you believe?
You will see greater things than these." 51 And He
*said to him, "Truly, truly, I say to you, you will
see THE HEAVENS OPENED AND THE ANGELS OF GOD
ASCENDING AND DESCENDING on the Son of Man."

The Wedding at Cana

2 And on the third day there was a wedding in
Cana of Galilee, and the mother of Jesus was
there; 2 and both Jesus and His disciples were
invited to the wedding. 3 And when the wine ran
out, the mother of Jesus *said to Him, "They
have no wine." 4 And Jesus *said to her, "Woman,
what do I have to do with you? My hour has not
yet come." 5 His mother *said to the servants,
"Whatever He says to you, do *it*." 6 Now there were
six stone water jars set there for the Jewish custom
of purification, containing [a]two or three measures

a. Approx. 20-30 gal. or 75-115 l, a measure was approx. 10 gal. or 38 l

each. 7 Jesus *said to them, "Fill the water jars with
water." So they filled them up to the brim. 8 And
He *said to them, "Draw *some* out now and take
it to the headwaiter." So they took it *to him*. 9 Now
when the headwaiter tasted the water which had
become wine, and did not know where it came
from (but the servants who had drawn the water
knew), the headwaiter *called the bridegroom,
10 and *said to him, "Every man serves the good
wine first, and when *the people* have drunk freely,
then the inferior *wine*; *but* you have kept the good
wine until now." 11 Jesus did this in Cana of Galilee
as the beginning of *His* signs, and manifested His
glory, and His disciples believed in Him.

12 After this He went down to Capernaum, He and His mother and *His* brothers and His disciples; and they stayed there a few days.

Jesus Cleanses the Temple

13 And the Passover of the Jews was near, and
Jesus went up to Jerusalem. 14 And He found in the
temple those who were selling oxen and sheep
and doves, and the money changers seated *at
their tables*. 15 And He made a scourge of cords,

and drove *them* all out of the temple, with the
sheep and the oxen; and He poured out the coins
of the money changers and overturned their
tables; 16 and to those who were selling the doves
He said, "Take these things away; stop making My
Father's house a place of business." 17 His disciples
remembered that it was written, "ZEAL FOR YOUR
HOUSE WILL CONSUME ME." 18 The Jews then said to
Him, "What sign do You show us as your authority
for doing these things?" 19 Jesus answered them,
"Destroy this sanctuary, and in three days I will
raise it up." 20 The Jews then said, "It took forty-six
years to build this sanctuary, and will You raise
it up in three days?" 21 But He was speaking about
the sanctuary of His body. 22 So when He was
raised from the dead, His disciples remembered
that He said this; and they believed the Scripture
and the word which Jesus had spoken.

23 Now when He was in Jerusalem at the
Passover, during the feast, many believed in His
name, when they saw His signs which He was
doing. 24 But Jesus, on His part, was not entrust-
ing Himself to them, for He knew all men, 25 and
because He had no need that anyone bear witness

concerning man, for He Himself knew what was
in man.

You Must Be Born Again

3 Now there was a man of the Pharisees, named
Nicodemus, a ruler of the Jews; 2 this man
came to Jesus by night and said to Him, “Rabbi, we
know that You have come from God *as* a teacher;
for no one can do these signs that You do unless
God is with him.” 3 Jesus answered and said to
him, “Truly, truly, I say to you, unless one is born
again he cannot see the kingdom of God.”
4 Nicodemus *said to Him, “How can a man be
born when he is old? Can he enter a second time
into his mother’s womb and be born?” 5 Jesus
answered, “Truly, truly, I say to you, unless one is
born of water and the Spirit he cannot enter into
the kingdom of God. 6 That which has been born
of the flesh is flesh, and that which has been born
of the Spirit is spirit. 7 Do not marvel that I said to
you, ‘You must be born again.’ 8 The wind blows
where it wishes and you hear its sound, but do not
know where it comes from and where it is going;
so is everyone who has been born of the Spirit.”

9 Nicodemus answered and said to Him, "How
can these things be?" 10 Jesus answered and said
to him, "Are you the teacher of Israel and do not
understand these things? 11 Truly, truly, I say to
you, we speak of what we know and bear wit-
ness of what we have seen, and you do not accept
our witness. 12 If I told you earthly things and you
do not believe, how will you believe if I tell you
heavenly things? 13 And no one has ascended into
heaven, but He who descended from heaven, the
Son of Man. 14 And as Moses lifted up the serpent
in the wilderness, even so must the Son of Man be
lifted up; 15 so that whoever believes will in Him
have eternal life.

16 "For God so loved the world, that He gave His
only begotten Son, that whoever believes in Him
shall not perish, but have eternal life. 17 For God
did not send the Son into the world to judge the
world, but that the world might be saved through
Him. 18 He who believes in Him is not judged; he
who does not believe has been judged already,
because he has not believed in the name of the
only begotten Son of God. 19 And this is the judg-
ment, that the Light has come into the world, and

men loved the darkness rather than the Light, for
their deeds were evil. [20] For everyone who does evil
hates the Light, and does not come to the Light
lest his deeds be exposed. [21] But he who practices
the truth comes to the Light, so that his deeds may
be manifested as having been done by God."

John the Baptist's Last Witness

[22] After these things Jesus and His disciples came
into the land of Judea, and there He was spending
time with them and baptizing. [23] And John also
was baptizing in Aenon near Salim, because there
was much water there; and *people* were coming
and were being baptized— [24] for John had not yet
been thrown into prison.

[25] Therefore there arose a debate between John's
disciples and a Jew about purification. [26] And they
came to John and said to him, "Rabbi, He who was
with you beyond the Jordan, to whom you have
borne witness, behold, He is baptizing and all
are coming to Him." [27] John answered and said, "A
man can receive nothing unless it has been given
him from heaven. [28] You yourselves are my wit-
nesses that I said, 'I am not the Christ,' but, 'I have

been sent ahead of Him.' [29] He who has the bride
is the bridegroom; but the friend of the bride-
groom, who stands and hears him, rejoices greatly
because of the bridegroom's voice. So this joy of
mine has been made full. [30] He must increase, but
I must decrease.

[31] "He who comes from above is above all, he
who is of the earth is from the earth and speaks
of the earth. He who comes from heaven is above
all. [32] What He has seen and heard, of that He
bears witness; and no one receives His witness.
[33] He who has received His witness has set his seal
to *this*, that God is true. [34] For He whom God has
sent speaks the words of God; for He gives the
Spirit without measure. [35] The Father loves the
Son and has given all things into His hand. [36] He
who believes in the Son has eternal life; but he
who does not obey the Son will not see life, but
the wrath of God abides on him."

Jesus Goes to Galilee

4 Therefore when Jesus knew that the Pharisees
had heard that Jesus was making and bap-
tizing more disciples than John [2] (although Jesus

Himself was not baptizing, but His disciples
were), [3]He left Judea and went away again into
Galilee. [4]And He had to pass through Samaria.
[5]So He *came to a city of Samaria called Sychar,
near the field that Jacob gave to his son Joseph;
[6]and Jacob's well was there. So Jesus, being wea-
ried from His journey, was sitting thus by the
well. It was about the sixth hour.

Jesus and the Samaritan Woman

[7]A woman of Samaria *came to draw water.
Jesus *said to her, "Give Me a drink." [8]For His dis-
ciples had gone away into the city to buy food.
[9]Therefore the Samaritan woman *said to Him,
"How do You, being a Jew, ask for a drink from me,
being a Samaritan woman?" (For Jews have no
dealings with Samaritans.) [10]Jesus answered and
said to her, "If you knew the gift of God, and who
it is who says to you, 'Give Me a drink,' you would
have asked Him, and He would have given you liv-
ing water." [11]She *said to Him, "Sir, You have noth-
ing to draw with and the well is deep. Where then
do You get that living water? [12]Are You greater
than our father Jacob, who gave us this well, and

drank of it himself and his sons and his cattle?”
13 Jesus answered and said to her, “Everyone who
drinks of this water will thirst again; 14 but who-
ever drinks of the water that I will give him will
never thirst—ever; but the water that I will give
him will become in him a well of water springing
up to eternal life.”
15 The woman *said to Him, “Sir, give me this
water, so I will not be thirsty nor come *back* here
to draw.” 16 He *said to her, “Go, call your husband
and come *back* here.” 17 The woman answered and
said, “I have no husband.” Jesus *said to her, “You
have correctly said, ‘I have no husband’; 18 for you
had five husbands, and the one you now have is
not your husband; this you have said truly.” 19 The
woman *said to Him, “Sir, I see that You are a
prophet. 20 Our fathers worshiped on this moun-
tain, and you *people* say that in Jerusalem is the
place where men ought to worship.” 21 Jesus *said
to her, “Woman, believe Me, an hour is coming
when neither in this mountain nor in Jerusalem
will you worship the Father. 22 You worship what
you do not know; we worship what we know,
for salvation is from the Jews. 23 But an hour is

coming, and now is, when the true worshipers
will worship the Father in spirit and truth; for
such people the Father seeks to be His worship-
ers. 24 God is spirit, and those who worship Him
must worship in spirit and truth." 25 The woman
*said to Him, "I know that Messiah is coming (He
who is called Christ); when He comes, He will
declare all things to us." 26 Jesus *said to her, "I
who speak to you am *He*."

27 And at this point His disciples came, and
they were marveling that He was speaking with
a woman, yet no one said, "What do You seek?"
or, "Why are You speaking with her?" 28 So the
woman left her water jar, and went into the city
and *said to the men, 29 "Come, see a man who
told me all the things that I *have* done; is this not
the Christ?" 30 They went out of the city, and were
coming to Him.

31 Meanwhile the disciples were urging Him,
saying, "Rabbi, eat." 32 But He said to them, "I have
food to eat that you do not know about." 33 So the
disciples were saying to one another, "Has any-
one brought Him *anything* to eat?" 34 Jesus *said
to them, "My food is to do the will of Him who

sent Me and to finish His work. 35 Do you not say,
'There are yet four months, and *then* comes the
harvest'? Behold, I say to you, lift up your eyes
and look on the fields, that they are white for har-
vest. 36 Even now he who reaps is receiving wages
and is gathering fruit for life eternal; so that he
who sows and he who reaps may rejoice together.
37 For in this *case* the saying is true, 'One sows and
another reaps.' 38 I sent you to reap that for which
you have not labored; others have labored and
you have entered into their labor."

Many Samaritans Believe

39 From that city many of the Samaritans
believed in Him because of the word of the woman
who bore witness, "He told me all the things that
I *have* done." 40 So when the Samaritans came to
Jesus, they were asking Him to stay with them;
and He stayed there two days. 41 And many more
believed because of His word; 42 and they were
saying to the woman, "It is no longer because of
what you said that we believe, for we have heard
for ourselves and know that this One is truly the
Savior of the world."

43 And after the two days He went from there
into Galilee. 44 For Jesus Himself bore witness that
a prophet has no honor in his own country. 45 So
when He came to Galilee, the Galileans received
Him, having seen all the things that He did in
Jerusalem at the feast; for they themselves also
went to the feast.

Jesus Heals a Royal Official's Son

46 Then He came again to Cana of Galilee where
He had made the water wine. And there was a
royal official whose son was sick at Capernaum.
47 When he heard that Jesus had come out of
Judea into Galilee, he went to Him and was ask-
ing *Him* to come down and heal his son; for he
was about to die. 48 So Jesus said to him, "Unless
you *people* see signs and wonders, you will never
believe." 49 The royal official *said to Him, "Sir,
come down before my child dies." 50 Jesus *said
to him, "Go; your son lives." The man believed
the word that Jesus spoke to him and started on
his way. 51 And while he was still going down, his
slaves met him, saying that his son was alive. 52 So
he inquired of them the hour when he began to

get better. Then they said to him, "Yesterday at the seventh hour the fever left him." 53 So the father knew that *it was* at that hour in which Jesus said to him, "Your son lives"; and he himself believed and his whole household. 54 This is again a second sign that Jesus did when He had come out of Judea into Galilee.

The Healing at Bethesda

5 After these things there was a feast of the Jews, and Jesus went up to Jerusalem.

2 Now there is in Jerusalem by the sheep *gate* a pool, which is called in Hebrew Bethesda, having five porticoes. 3 In these lay a multitude of those who were sick, blind, lame, and withered, [waiting for the moving of the waters; 4 for an angel of the Lord went down at certain seasons into the pool and stirred up the water; whoever then first, after the stirring up of the water, stepped in was made well from whatever sickness with which he was afflicted.] 5 And a man was there who had been sick for thirty-eight years. 6 When Jesus saw him lying *there* and knew that he had already been *sick* a long time, He *said to him, "Do you

wish to get well?" 7 The sick man answered Him,
"Sir, I have no man to put me into the pool when
the water is stirred up, but while I am coming,
another steps down before me." 8 Jesus *said to
him, "Get up, pick up your mat and walk." 9 And
immediately the man became well, and picked up
his mat and *began to* walk.

Now it was the Sabbath on that day. 10 So the
Jews were saying to the man who had been
healed, "It is the Sabbath, and it is not lawful for
you to carry your mat." 11 But he answered them,
"He who made me well was the one who said to
me, 'Pick up your mat and walk.' " 12 They asked
him, "Who is the man who said to you, 'Pick up
your mat and walk'?" 13 But the man who was
healed did not know who it was, for Jesus had
slipped away while there was a crowd in *that*
place. 14 Afterward Jesus *found him in the temple
and said to him, "Behold, you have become well;
do not sin anymore, so that nothing worse hap-
pens to you." 15 The man went away, and disclosed
to the Jews that it was Jesus who had made him
well. 16 And for this reason the Jews were persecut-
ing Jesus, because He was doing these things on

the Sabbath. [17] But He answered them, "My Father
is working until now, and I Myself am working."

Jesus' Equality with the Father

[18] For this reason therefore the Jews were seeking
all the more to kill Him, because He not only was
breaking the Sabbath, but also was calling God
His own Father, making Himself equal with God.
[19] Therefore Jesus answered and was saying to
them, "Truly, truly, I say to you, the Son can do
nothing from Himself, unless *it is* something He
sees the Father doing; for whatever the Father
does, these things the Son also does in the same
manner. [20] For the Father loves the Son, and shows
Him all things that He Himself is doing; and *the
Father* will show Him greater works than these, so
that you will marvel. [21] For just as the Father raises
the dead and gives *them* life, even so the Son also
gives life to whom He wishes. [22] For not even the
Father judges anyone, but He has given all judg-
ment to the Son, [23] so that all will honor the Son
even as they honor the Father. He who does not
honor the Son does not honor the Father who
sent Him.

24 "Truly, truly, I say to you, he who hears My
word, and believes Him who sent Me, has eternal
life, and does not come into judgment, but has
passed out of death into life.

Two Resurrections

25 Truly, truly, I say to you, an hour is coming and
now is, when the dead will hear the voice of the
Son of God, and those who hear will live. 26 For
just as the Father has life in Himself, even so He
gave to the Son also to have life in Himself; 27 and
He gave Him authority to execute judgment,
because He is the Son of Man. 28 Do not marvel at
this; for an hour is coming, in which all who are
in the tombs will hear His voice, 29 and will come
forth; those who did the good deeds to a resurrec-
tion of life, those who committed the evil deeds
to a resurrection of judgment.

30 "I can do nothing from Myself. As I hear, I
judge; and My judgment is righteous, because I
do not seek My own will, but the will of Him who
sent Me.

31 "If I *alone* bear witness about Myself, My wit-
ness is not true. 32 There is another who bears

witness about Me, and I know that the witness
which He gives about Me is true.

Witnesses to Jesus: The Father and the Scriptures

33 You have sent to John, and he has borne wit-
ness to the truth. 34 But the witness I receive is not
from man, but I say these things so that you may
be saved. 35 He was the lamp that was burning and
shining and you were willing to rejoice for a while
in his light. 36 But the witness I have is greater
than *the witness of* John; for the works which the
Father has given Me to finish—the very works
that I do—bear witness about Me, that the Father
has sent Me. 37 And the Father who sent Me, He has
borne witness about Me. You have neither heard
His voice at any time nor seen His form. 38 And
you do not have His word abiding in you, for you
do not believe Him whom He sent. 39 You search
the Scriptures because you think that in them
you have eternal life; it is these that bear witness
about Me; 40 and you are unwilling to come to Me
so that you may have life. 41 I do not receive glory
from men; 42 but I know you, that you do not have
the love of God in yourselves. 43 I have come in

My Father's name, and you do not receive Me; if
another comes in his own name, you will receive
him. 44 How can you believe, when you receive
glory from one another and you do not seek the
glory that is from the only God? 45 Do not think
that I will accuse you to the Father; the one who
accuses you is Moses, in whom you have set your
hope. 46 For if you believed Moses, you would
believe Me, for he wrote about Me. 47 But if you
do not believe his writings, how will you believe
My words?"

Jesus Feeds Five Thousand

6 After these things Jesus went away to the
other side of the Sea of Galilee (or Tiberias).
2 Now a large crowd was following Him, because
they were seeing the signs which He was doing
on those who were sick. 3 Then Jesus went up on
the mountain, and there He was sitting down
with His disciples. 4 Now the Passover, the feast
of the Jews, was near. 5 Therefore Jesus, lifting up
His eyes and seeing that a large crowd was com-
ing to Him, *said to Philip, "Where should we buy
bread, so that these people may eat?" 6 And this

He was saying to test him, for He Himself knew
what He was going to do. 7 Philip answered Him,
"Two hundred [b]denarii worth of bread is not suf-
ficient for them, for everyone to receive a little."
8 One of His disciples, Andrew, Simon Peter's
brother, *said to Him, 9 "There is a boy here who
has five barley loaves and two fish, but what are
these for so many people?" 10 Jesus said, "Have
the people sit down." Now there was much grass
in the place. So the men sat down, in number
about five thousand. 11 Jesus then took the loaves,
and having given thanks, He distributed *them* to
those who were seated; likewise also of the fish,
as much as they wanted. 12 And when they were
filled, He *said to His disciples, "Gather up the
leftover pieces so that nothing will be lost." 13 So
they gathered them up, and filled twelve baskets
with pieces of the five barley loaves left over by
those who had eaten. 14 Therefore when the peo-
ple saw the sign which He had done, they were
saying, "This is truly the Prophet who is to come
into the world."

---

b. A Roman silver coin, approx. a laborer's daily wage

Jesus Walks on the Sea

15 So Jesus, knowing that they were going to
come and take Him by force to make Him king,
withdrew again to the mountain by Himself alone.

16 Now when evening came, His disciples went
down to the sea, 17 and after getting into a boat, they
began to cross the sea to Capernaum. It had already
become dark, and Jesus had not yet come to them.
18 And the sea *was stirred up because a strong wind
was blowing. 19 Then, when they had rowed about
[c]twenty-five or thirty stadia, they *saw Jesus walk-
ing on the sea and drawing near to the boat; and
they were frightened. 20 But He *said to them, "It is
I; do not be afraid." 21 So they were willing to receive
Him into the boat, and immediately the boat was at
the land to which they were going.

22 On the next day, the crowd which stood on the
other side of the sea saw that there was no other
small boat there, except one, and that Jesus had
not entered with His disciples into the boat, but
that His disciples had gone away alone. 23 Other
small boats came from Tiberias near to the place
where they ate the bread after the Lord had given

c. Approx. 2.8-3.5 mi. or 4.6-5.5 km; a stadion was about 607 ft. or 185 m

thanks. 24 So when the crowd saw that Jesus was
not there, nor His disciples, they themselves got
into the small boats, and came to Capernaum
seeking Jesus. 25 And when they found Him on the
other side of the sea, they said to Him, “Rabbi,
when did You come here?”

I Am the Bread of Life

26 Jesus answered them and said, “Truly, truly,
I say to you, you seek Me, not because you saw
signs, but because you ate of the loaves and were
filled. 27 Do not work for the food which perishes,
but for the food which endures to eternal life,
which the Son of Man will give to you, for on Him
the Father, God, set His seal.” 28 Therefore they said
to Him, “What should we do, so that we may work
the works of God?” 29 Jesus answered and said to
them, “This is the work of God, that you believe
in Him whom He has sent.” 30 So they said to Him,
“What then do You do for a sign so that we may
see, and believe You? What work do You perform?
31 Our fathers ate the manna in the wilderness; as
it is written, ‘HE GAVE THEM BREAD FROM HEAVEN
TO EAT.’ ” 32 Jesus then said to them, “Truly, truly,

I say to you, Moses has not given you the bread
from heaven, but My Father gives you the true
bread from heaven. 33 For the bread of God is that
which comes down from heaven and gives life to
the world." 34 Then they said to Him, "Lord, always
give us this bread."

35 Jesus said to them, "I am the bread of life. He
who comes to Me will never hunger, and he who
believes in Me will never thirst. 36 But I said to you
that you have seen Me, and yet do not believe. 37 All
that the Father gives Me will come to Me, and the
one who comes to Me I will never cast out. 38 For I
have come down from heaven, not to do My own
will, but the will of Him who sent Me. 39 Now this
is the will of Him who sent Me, that of all that He
has given Me I lose nothing, but raise it up on the
last day. 40 For this is the will of My Father, that
everyone who sees the Son and believes in Him
will have eternal life, and I Myself will raise him
up on the last day."

Words to the Jews

41 Therefore the Jews were grumbling about Him,
because He said, "I am the bread that came down

from heaven." 42 They were saying, "Is not this
Jesus, the son of Joseph, whose father and mother
we know? How does He now say, 'I have come
down from heaven'?" 43 Jesus answered and said
to them, "Stop grumbling among yourselves. 44 No
one can come to Me unless the Father who sent Me
draws him; and I will raise him up on the last day.
45 It is written in the prophets, 'AND THEY SHALL ALL
BE TAUGHT BY GOD.' Everyone who has heard and
learned from the Father comes to Me. 46 Not that
anyone has seen the Father, except the One who
is from God; He has seen the Father. 47 Truly, truly,
I say to you, he who believes has eternal life. 48 I am
the bread of life. 49 Your fathers ate the manna in
the wilderness, and they died. 50 This is the bread
which comes down from heaven, so that one may
eat of it and not die. 51 I am the living bread that
came down from heaven; if anyone eats of this
bread, he will live forever; and also the bread which
I will give for the life of the world is My flesh."

52 Then the Jews *began to* argue with one
another, saying, "How can this man give us *His*
flesh to eat?" 53 So Jesus said to them, "Truly, truly,
I say to you, unless you eat the flesh of the Son

of Man and drink His blood, you have no life in
yourselves. [54] He who eats My flesh and drinks My
blood has eternal life, and I will raise him up on
the last day. [55] For My flesh is true food, and My
blood is true drink. [56] He who eats My flesh and
drinks My blood abides in Me, and I in him. [57] As
the living Father sent Me, and I live because of the
Father, so he who eats Me, he also will live because
of Me. [58] This is the bread which came down out of
heaven, not as the fathers ate and died. He who
eats this bread will live forever."

Words to the Disciples

59 These things He said in the synagogue as He
taught in Capernaum.

60 Therefore many of His disciples, when they
heard *this* said, "This is a difficult statement; who
can listen to it?" [61] But Jesus, knowing in Himself
that His disciples were grumbling at this, said to
them, "Does this cause you to stumble? [62] *What*
then if you see the Son of Man ascending to
where He was before? [63] The Spirit is the One who
gives life; the flesh profits nothing; the words that
I have spoken to you are spirit and are life. [64] But

there are some of you who do not believe." For
Jesus knew from the beginning who they were
who did not believe, and who it was that would
betray Him. 65 And He was saying, "For this reason
I have said to you, that no one can come to Me
unless it has been granted him from the Father."

Peter Confesses Jesus Is the Christ

66 As a result of this many of His disciples went
away and were not walking with Him anymore.
67 So Jesus said to the twelve, "Do you also want
to go?" 68 Simon Peter answered Him, "Lord, to
whom shall we go? You have words of eternal
life. 69 And we have believed and have come to
know that You are the Holy One of God." 70 Jesus
answered them, "Did I Myself not choose you, the
twelve, and *yet* one of you is a devil?" 71 Now He
was speaking of Judas *the son* of Simon Iscariot,
for he, one of the twelve, was going to betray Him.

Jesus Teaches at the Feast of Booths

7 And after these things Jesus was walking in
Galilee, for He was unwilling to walk in Judea
because the Jews were seeking to kill Him. 2 Now

the feast of the Jews, the Feast of Booths, was near.
3 Therefore His brothers said to Him, “Leave here
and go into Judea, so that Your disciples also may
see Your works which You are doing. 4 For no one
does anything in secret when he himself seeks
to be *known* openly. If You do these things, show
Yourself publicly to the world.” 5 For not even His
brothers were believing in Him. 6 So Jesus *said to
them, “My time is not yet here, but your time is
always here. 7 The world cannot hate you, but it
hates Me because I bear witness about it, that its
deeds are evil. 8 Go up to the feast yourselves; I am
not yet going up to this feast because My time has
not yet been fulfilled.” 9 Having said these things
to them, He stayed in Galilee.

10 But when His brothers had gone up to the
feast, then He Himself also went up, not publicly,
but as in secret. 11 So the Jews were seeking Him at
the feast and saying, “Where is He?” 12 And there
was much grumbling among the crowds concern-
ing Him; some were saying, “He is a good man”;
others were saying, “No, on the contrary, He
leads the crowd astray.” 13 Yet no one was speaking
openly about Him for fear of the Jews.

[14] But when it was now the middle of the feast
Jesus went up into the temple, and *began to* teach.
[15] The Jews then were marveling, saying, "How has
this man become learned, not having been edu-
cated?" [16] So Jesus answered them and said, "My
teaching is not Mine, but from Him who sent Me.
[17] If anyone is willing to do His will, he will know
about the teaching, whether it is of God or I speak
from Myself. [18] He who speaks from himself seeks
his own glory; but He who is seeking the glory of
the One who sent Him, He is true, and there is no
unrighteousness in Him.

[19] "Did not Moses give you the Law? And *yet*
none of you does the Law. Why do you seek to
kill Me?" [20] The crowd answered, "You have a
demon! Who seeks to kill You?" [21] Jesus answered
them, "I did one work, and you all marvel. [22] For
this reason Moses has given you circumcision
(not because it is from Moses, but from the
fathers), and on *the* Sabbath you circumcise a
man. [23] If a man receives circumcision on the
Sabbath so that the Law of Moses will not be
broken, are you angry with Me because I made
an entire man well on *the* Sabbath? [24] Do not

judge according to appearance, but judge with
righteous judgment."
25 So some of the people of Jerusalem were say-
ing, "Is this not the man whom they are seeking
to kill? 26 And look, He is speaking openly, and
they are saying nothing to Him. Do the rulers
truly know that this is the Christ? 27 However, we
know where this man is from; but whenever the
Christ comes, no one knows where He is from."
28 Then Jesus cried out in the temple, teaching
and saying, "You both know Me and know where
I am from; and I have not come of Myself, but
He who sent Me is true, whom you do not know.
29 I know Him, because I am from Him, and He
sent Me." 30 So they were seeking to seize Him;
yet no man laid his hand on Him, because His
hour had not yet come. 31 But many of the crowd
believed in Him; and they were saying, "When
the Christ comes, will He do more signs than this
man did?"
32 The Pharisees heard the crowd whispering
these things about Him, and the chief priests
and the Pharisees sent officers to seize Him.
33 Therefore Jesus said, "For a little while longer I

am with you, then I go to Him who sent Me. 34 You
will seek Me, and will not find Me; and where I
am, you cannot come." 35 The Jews then said to
one another, "Where does this man intend to go
that we will not find Him? Is He intending to go
to the Dispersion among the Greeks and teach
the Greeks? 36 What is this statement that He said,
'You will seek Me, and will not find Me; and where
I am, you cannot come'?"

37 Now on the last day, the great *day* of the feast,
Jesus stood and cried out, saying, "If anyone is
thirsty, let him come to Me and drink. 38 He who
believes in Me, as the Scripture said, 'From his
innermost being will flow rivers of living water.' "
39 But this He spoke of the Spirit, whom those who
believed in Him were going to receive; for the
Spirit was not yet *given*, because Jesus was not
yet glorified.

Division of People over Jesus

40 *Some* of the crowd therefore, when they
heard these words, were saying, "This truly is
the Prophet." 41 Others were saying, "This is the
Christ." Still others were saying, "*No*, for is the

Christ going to come from Galilee? [42] Has not the
Scripture said that the Christ comes from the seed
of David and from Bethlehem, the village where
David was?" [43] So a division occurred in the crowd
because of Him. [44] Some of them were wanting to
seize Him, but no one laid hands on Him.

[45] The officers then came to the chief priests and
Pharisees, and they said to them, "Why did you
not bring Him?" [46] The officers answered, "Never
has a man spoken like this!" [47] The Pharisees then
answered them, "Have you also been led astray?
[48] Have any of the rulers or Pharisees believed in
Him? [49] But this crowd which does not know the
Law is accursed." [50] Nicodemus (he who came to
Him before), being one of them, *said to them,
[51] "Does our Law judge a man unless it first hears
from him and knows what he is doing?" [52] They
answered him, "Are you also from Galilee? Search
and see that no prophet arises out of Galilee."
[53] [Everyone went to his home.

An Adulteress Forgiven

8 But Jesus went to the Mount of Olives. [2] Early
in the morning He came again into the

temple, and all the people were coming to Him;
and He sat down and *began to* teach them. 3 The
scribes and the Pharisees *brought a woman
caught in adultery, and having set her in the
center *of the court*, 4 they *said to Him, “Teacher,
this woman has been caught in adultery, in the
very act. 5 Now in the Law Moses commanded us
to stone such women; what then do You say?”
6 They were saying this, testing Him, so that they
might have *evidence* to accuse Him. But Jesus
stooped down and with His finger wrote on
the ground. 7 But when they persisted in asking
Him, He straightened up and said to them, “Let
him who is without sin among you *be the* first to
throw a stone at her.” 8 Again He stooped down
and wrote on the ground. 9 When they heard
it, they began *to* go out one by one, beginning
with the older ones, and He was left alone, and
the woman, where she was, in the center *of
the court*. 10 Straightening up, Jesus said to her,
“Woman, where are they? Did no one condemn
you?” 11 She said, “No one, Lord.” And Jesus said, “I
do not condemn you, either. Go, and from now on
sin no more.”]

I Am the Light of the World

12 Then Jesus again spoke to them, saying, "I
am the Light of the world; he who follows Me
will never walk in the darkness, but will have the
Light of life." 13 So the Pharisees said to Him, "You
are bearing witness about Yourself; Your witness
is not true." 14 Jesus answered and said to them,
"Even if I bear witness about Myself, My witness
is true, for I know where I came from and where I
am going; but you do not know where I come from
or where I am going. 15 You judge according to the
flesh; I am not judging anyone. 16 But even if I do
judge, My judgment is true; for I am not alone *in
it*, but I and the Father who sent Me. 17 Even in your
law it has been written that the witness of two
men is true. 18 I am He who bears witness about
Myself, and the Father who sent Me bears witness
about Me." 19 So they were saying to Him, "Where
is Your Father?" Jesus answered, "You know nei-
ther Me nor My Father; if you knew Me, you would
know My Father also." 20 These words He spoke in
the treasury, as He was teaching in the temple;
and no one seized Him, because His hour had not
yet come.

21 Then He said again to them, "I am going away,
and you will seek Me, and will die in your sin.
Where I am going, you cannot come." 22 So the
Jews were saying, "Surely He will not kill Himself,
since He says, 'Where I am going, you cannot
come'?" 23 And He was saying to them, "You are
from below, I am from above. You are of this
world, I am not of this world. 24 Therefore I said to
you that you will die in your sins. For unless you
believe that I am *He*, you will die in your sins." 25 So
they were saying to Him, "Who are You?" Jesus
said to them, "What have I been saying to you
from the beginning? 26 I have many things to say
and to judge concerning you, but He who sent Me
is true; and the things which I heard from Him,
these I am saying to the world." 27 They did not
know that He had been speaking to them about
the Father. 28 So Jesus said, "When you lift up the
Son of Man, then you will know that I am *He*, and
I do nothing from Myself, but I speak these things
as the Father taught Me. 29 And He who sent Me is
with Me; He has not left Me alone, for I always do
the things that are pleasing to Him." 30 As He was
speaking these things, many believed in Him.

The Son Will Make You Free

[31]So Jesus was saying to those Jews who had
believed Him, "If you abide in My word, *then* you
are truly My disciples; [32]and you will know the
truth, and the truth will make you free." [33]They
answered Him, "We are Abraham's seed and have
never yet been enslaved to anyone. How is it that
You say, 'You will become free'?"

[34]Jesus answered them, "Truly, truly, I say to
you, everyone who commits sin is the slave of
sin. [35]And the slave does not remain in the house
forever; the son does remain forever. [36]So if the
Son makes you free, you will be free indeed. [37]I
know that you are Abraham's seed; yet you are
seeking to kill Me, because My word has no place
in you. [38]I speak the things which I have seen with
My Father; therefore you also do the things which
you heard from *your* father."

[39]They answered and said to Him, "Abraham
is our father." Jesus *said to them, "If you are
Abraham's children, you would do the deeds of
Abraham. [40]But now you are seeking to kill Me,
a man who has told you the truth, which I heard
from God. This Abraham did not do. [41]You are

doing the deeds of your father." They said to
Him, "We were not born of sexual immorality;
we have one Father: God." 42 Jesus said to them,
"If God were your Father, you would love Me, for
I proceeded forth and have come from God, for
I have not even come of Myself, but He sent Me.
43 Why do you not understand what I am saying?
It is because you cannot hear My word. 44 You are
of *your* father the devil, and you want to do the
desires of your father. He was a murderer from
the beginning, and does not stand in the truth
because there is no truth in him. Whenever he
speaks a lie, he speaks from his own *nature*, for
he is a liar and the father of lies. 45 But because I
speak the truth, you do not believe Me. 46 Which
one of you convicts Me of sin? If I speak truth,
why do you not believe Me? 47 He who is of God
hears the words of God; for this reason you do not
hear *them*, because you are not of God."

48 The Jews answered and said to Him, "Do we
not say rightly that You are a Samaritan and have a
demon?" 49 Jesus answered, "I do not have a demon,
but I honor My Father, and you dishonor Me. 50 But
I do not seek My glory; there is One who seeks and

judges. 51 Truly, truly, I say to you, if anyone keeps
My word he will never see death—ever." 52 The Jews
said to Him, "Now we know that You have a demon.
Abraham died, and the prophets *also*; and You
say, 'If anyone keeps My word, he will never taste
of death—ever.' 53 Surely You are not greater than
our father Abraham who died? The prophets died
too; whom do You make Yourself out *to be*?" 54 Jesus
answered, "If I glorify Myself, My glory is nothing;
it is My Father who glorifies Me, of whom you say,
'He is our God'; 55 and you have not known Him, but
I know Him; and if I say that I do not know Him, I
will be a liar like you, but I do know Him and keep
His word. 56 Your father Abraham rejoiced to see My
day, and he saw *it* and was glad." 57 So the Jews said
to Him, "You are not yet fifty years old, and have
You seen Abraham?" 58 Jesus said to them, "Truly,
truly, I say to you, before Abraham was, I am."
59 Therefore they picked up stones to throw at Him,
but Jesus hid Himself and went out of the temple.

Jesus Heals a Man Born Blind

9 As He passed by, He saw a man blind from
birth. 2 And His disciples asked Him, saying,

"Rabbi, who sinned, this man or his parents,
that he would be born blind?" 3 Jesus answered,
"Neither this man nor his parents sinned, but
this was so that the works of God might be man-
ifested in him. 4 We must work the works of Him
who sent Me as long as it is day; night is coming
when no one can work. 5 While I am in the world,
I am the light of the world." 6 When He had said
this, He spat on the ground, made clay of the
saliva, and rubbed the clay on his eyes, 7 and said
to him, "Go, wash in the pool of Siloam" (which
is translated, Sent). So he went away and washed,
and came *back* seeing. 8 Therefore the neighbors,
and those who previously saw him as a beggar,
were saying, "Is not this the one who used to sit
and beg?" 9 Others were saying, "This is he," *still*
others were saying, "No, but he is like him." He
kept saying, "I am the one." 10 So they were say-
ing to him, "How then were your eyes opened?"
11 He answered, "The man who is called Jesus
made clay, and rubbed my eyes, and said to me,
'Go to Siloam and wash'; so when I went away and
washed, I received sight." 12 And they said to him,
"Where is He?" He *said, "I do not know."

Controversy over the Man Born Blind

[13] They *brought to the Pharisees the man who
was formerly blind. [14] Now it was a Sabbath on
the day when Jesus made the clay and opened
his eyes. [15] So the Pharisees also were asking him
again how he received his sight. And he said to
them, "He applied clay to my eyes, and I washed,
and I see." [16] So then some of the Pharisees were
saying, "This man is not from God, because He
does not keep the Sabbath." But others were saying, "How can a sinful man do such signs?" And
there was a division among them. [17] Therefore,
they *said to the blind man again, "What do you
say about Him, since He opened your eyes?" And
he said, "He is a prophet."

[18] Then, the Jews did not believe *it* of him that he
was blind and had received sight, until they called
the parents of the very one who had received
his sight, [19] and questioned them, saying, "Is this
your son, who you say was born blind? Then how
does he now see?" [20] So his parents answered and
said, "We know that this is our son, and that he
was born blind; [21] but how he now sees, we do not
know; or who opened his eyes, we do not know.

Ask him; he is of age, he will speak for himself."
22 His parents said this because they were afraid
of the Jews; for the Jews had already agreed that
if anyone confessed Him to be Christ, he was to
be put out of the synagogue. 23 For this reason his
parents said, "He is of age; ask him."
24 Therefore, a second time they called the man
who had been blind, and said to him, "Give glory
to God; we know that this man is a sinner." 25 He
then answered, "Whether He is a sinner, I do not
know; one thing I do know, that though I was
blind, now I see." 26 So they said to him, "What
did He do to you? How did He open your eyes?"
27 He answered them, "I told you already and you
did not listen. Why do you want to listen again?
Do you want to become His disciples too?" 28 And
they reviled him and said, "You are His disciple,
but we are disciples of Moses. 29 We know that God
has spoken to Moses, but as for this man, we do
not know where He is from." 30 The man answered
and said to them, "Well, here is a marvelous thing,
that you do not know where He is from, and He
opened my eyes. 31 We know that God does not lis-
ten to sinners; but if anyone is God-fearing and

does His will, He listens to him. 32 Since the begin-
ning of time it has never been heard that anyone
opened the eyes of a person born blind. 33 If this
man were not from God, He could do nothing."
34 They answered and said to him, "You were born
entirely in sins, and are you teaching us?" So they
put him out.

Jesus Affirms His Deity

35 Jesus heard that they had put him out, and
after finding him, He said, "Do you believe in
the Son of Man?" 36 He answered and said, "Who
is He, Lord, that I may believe in Him?" 37 Jesus
said to him, "You have both seen Him, and He is
the one who is talking with you." 38 And he said,
"Lord, I believe." And he worshiped Him. 39 And
Jesus said, "For judgment I came into this world,
so that those who do not see may see, and that
those who see may become blind." 40 Some of the
Pharisees who were with Him heard these things
and said to Him, "Are we blind too?" 41 Jesus said
to them, "If you were blind, you would have
no sin; but now *that* you say, 'We see,' your sin
remains.

I Am the Good Shepherd

10 “Truly, truly, I say to you, he who does not
enter by the door into the fold of the sheep,
but climbs up some other way, he is a thief and a
robber. 2 But he who enters by the door is a shep-
herd of the sheep. 3 To him the doorkeeper opens,
and the sheep hear his voice, and he calls his
own sheep by name and leads them out. 4 When
he brings all his own out, he goes ahead of them,
and the sheep follow him because they know
his voice. 5 A stranger they will never follow, but
will flee from him, because they do not know the
voice of strangers.” 6 This figure of speech Jesus
spoke to them, but they did not understand what
those things were which He had been saying to
them.

7 So Jesus said to them again, “Truly, truly, I say
to you, I am the door of the sheep. 8 All who came
before Me are thieves and robbers, but the sheep
did not hear them. 9 I am the door; if anyone
enters through Me, he will be saved, and will go in
and out and find pasture. 10 The thief comes only
to steal and kill and destroy; I came that they may
have life, and have *it* abundantly.

11 "I am the good shepherd; the good shep-
herd lays down His life for the sheep. 12 He who
is a hired hand, and not a shepherd, who is not
the owner of the sheep, sees the wolf coming,
and leaves the sheep and flees—and the wolf
snatches and scatters them— 13 because he is
a hired hand and is not concerned about the
sheep. 14 I am the good shepherd, and I know My
own and My own know Me, 15 even as the Father
knows Me and I know the Father; and I lay down
My life for the sheep. 16 And I have other sheep,
which are not from this fold; I must bring them
also, and they will hear My voice; and they will
become one flock *with* one shepherd. 17 For this
reason the Father loves Me, because I lay down
My life so that I may take it again. 18 No one takes
it away from Me, but from Myself, I lay it down. I
have authority to lay it down, and I have author-
ity to take it up again. This commandment I
received from My Father."

19 A division occurred again among the Jews
because of these words. 20 And many of them
were saying, "He has a demon and is insane.
Why do you listen to Him?" 21 Others were

saying, "These are not the words of someone demon-possessed. Can a demon open the eyes of the blind?"

I and the Father Are One

22 At that time the Feast of the Dedication took
place at Jerusalem; 23 it was winter, and Jesus was
walking in the temple in the Portico of Solomon.
24 The Jews then gathered around Him, and were
saying to Him, "How long will You keep us in
suspense? If You are the Christ, tell us openly."
25 Jesus answered them, "I told you, and you do
not believe; the works that I do in My Father's
name, these bear witness of Me. 26 But you do not
believe because you are not of My sheep. 27 My
sheep hear My voice, and I know them, and they
follow Me; 28 and I give eternal life to them, and
they will never perish—ever; and no one will
snatch them out of My hand. 29 My Father, who
has given *them* to Me, is greater than all; and
no one is able to snatch *them* out of the Father's
hand. 30 I and the Father are one."

31 The Jews picked up stones again to stone
Him. 32 Jesus answered them, "I showed you

many good works from the Father; for which of
them are you stoning Me?" [33] The Jews answered
Him, "For a good work we do not stone You, but
for blasphemy; and because You, being a man,
make Yourself God." [34] Jesus answered them,
"Has it not been written in your Law, 'I SAID, YOU
ARE GODS'? [35] If he called them gods, to whom the
word of God came (and the Scripture cannot be
broken), [36] do you say of Him, whom the Father
sanctified and sent into the world, 'You are blas-
pheming,' because I said, 'I am the Son of God'?
[37] If I do not do the works of My Father, do not
believe Me; [38] but if I do them, though you do not
believe Me, believe the works, so that you may
know and continue knowing that the Father
is in Me, and I in the Father." [39] Therefore they
were seeking again to seize Him, and He eluded
their grasp.

[40] And He went away again beyond the Jordan
to the place where John was first baptizing, and
He was staying there. [41] And many came to Him
and were saying, "While John did no sign, yet
everything John said about this man was true."
[42] And many believed in Him there.

The Death and Resurrection of Lazarus

11 Now a certain man was sick, Lazarus from
Bethany, the village of Mary and her sister
Martha. 2 And it was *the* Mary who anointed the
Lord with perfume, and wiped His feet with her
hair, whose brother Lazarus was sick. 3 So the sis-
ters sent to Him, saying, "Lord, behold, he whom
You love is sick." 4 But when Jesus heard *this*, He
said, "This sickness is not to end in death, but is
for the glory of God, so that the Son of God may
be glorified by it." 5 Now Jesus loved Martha and
her sister and Lazarus. 6 So when He heard that
he was sick, He then stayed two days in the place
where He was. 7 Then after this He *said to the
disciples, "Let us go to Judea again." 8 The disci-
ples *said to Him, "Rabbi, the Jews were just now
seeking to stone You, and are You going there
again?" 9 Jesus answered, "Are there not twelve
hours in the day? If anyone walks in the day, he
does not stumble, because he sees the light of
this world. 10 But if anyone walks in the night, he
stumbles, because the light is not in him." 11 He
said these things, and after that He *said to them,
"Our friend Lazarus has fallen asleep; but I go, so

that I may awaken him." 12 The disciples then said
to Him, "Lord, if he has fallen asleep, he will be
saved *from his sickness*." 13 Now Jesus had spoken
of his death, but they thought that He was speak-
ing of actual sleep. 14 So Jesus then said to them
plainly, "Lazarus is dead, 15 and I am glad for your
sakes that I was not there, so that you may believe;
but let us go to him." 16 Therefore Thomas, who is
called Didymus, said to *his* fellow disciples, "Let
us also go, so that we may die with Him."

17 So when Jesus came, He found that he had
already been in the tomb four days. 18 Now
Bethany was near Jerusalem, about [d]fifteen stadia
away; 19 and many of the Jews had come to Martha
and Mary, to console them about their brother.
20 Martha therefore, when she heard that Jesus
was coming, went to meet Him, but Mary was
sitting in the house. 21 Martha then said to Jesus,
"Lord, if You had been here, my brother would not
have died. 22 But even now I know that whatever
You ask from God, God will give You." 23 Jesus *said
to her, "Your brother will rise again." 24 Martha
*said to Him, "I know that he will rise again in the

---

d. Approx. 1.7 mi. or 2.7 km, a stadion was approx. 607 ft. or 185 m

resurrection on the last day." 25 Jesus said to her, "I
am the resurrection and the life; he who believes
in Me will live even if he dies, 26 and everyone who
lives and believes in Me will never die—ever. Do
you believe this?" 27 She *said to Him, "Yes, Lord;
I have believed that You are the Christ, the Son of
God, the One who comes into the world."

28 And when she had said this, she went away
and called Mary her sister, saying secretly, "The
Teacher is here and is calling for you." 29 And
when she heard it, she *got up quickly and was
coming to Him.

30 Now Jesus had not yet come into the village,
but was still in the place where Martha met Him.
31 Then the Jews—who were with her in the house
and consoling her—when they saw that Mary
rose up quickly and went out, they followed her,
thinking that she was going to the tomb to cry
there. 32 Therefore, when Mary came where Jesus
was, she saw Him, and fell at His feet, saying to
Him, "Lord, if You had been here, my brother
would not have died." 33 When Jesus therefore saw
her crying, and the Jews who came with her *also*
crying, He was deeply moved in spirit and was

troubled, 34 and said, "Where have you laid him?"
They *said to Him, "Lord, come and see." 35 Jesus
wept. 36 So the Jews were saying, "See how He
loved him!" 37 But some of them said, "Could not
this man, who opened the eyes of the blind man,
have kept this man also from dying?"

38 So Jesus, again being deeply moved within,
*came to the tomb. Now it was a cave, and a stone
was lying against it. 39 Jesus *said, "Remove the
stone." Martha, the sister of the deceased, *said
to Him, "Lord, by this time he smells, for he has
been *dead* four days." 40 Jesus *said to her, "Did I
not say to you that if you believe, you will see the
glory of God?" 41 So they removed the stone. Then
Jesus raised His eyes, and said, "Father, I thank
You that You have heard Me. 42 And I knew that You
always hear Me; but because of the crowd standing around I said this, so that they may believe
that You sent Me." 43 And when He had said these
things, He cried out with a loud voice, "Lazarus,
come forth." 44 The man who had died came forth,
bound hand and foot with wrappings, and his
face was wrapped around with a cloth. Jesus *said
to them, "Unbind him, and let him go."

45 Therefore many of the Jews who came to Mary,
and saw what He had done, believed in Him. 46 But
some of them went to the Pharisees and told them
the things which Jesus had done.

The Leaders Plot to Kill Jesus

47 Therefore the chief priests and the Pharisees
gathered the Sanhedrin together, and were say-
ing, "What are we doing? For this man is doing
many signs. 48 If we let Him *go on* like this, all will
believe in Him, and the Romans will come and
take away both our place and our nation." 49 But
one of them, Caiaphas, who was high priest that
year, said to them, "You know nothing at all, 50 nor
do you take into account that it is better for you
that one man should die for the people, and that
the whole nation not perish." 51 Now he did not
say this from himself, but being high priest that
year, he prophesied that Jesus was going to die for
the nation, 52 and not for the nation only, but in
order that He might also gather together into one
the children of God who are scattered abroad.
53 So from that day on they planned together to
kill Him.

54 Therefore Jesus no longer continued to walk
openly among the Jews, but went away from there
to the region near the wilderness, into a city called
Ephraim; and there He stayed with the disciples.
55 Now the Passover of the Jews was near, and
many went up to Jerusalem from the region before
the Passover to purify themselves. 56 So they were
seeking Jesus, and were saying to one another as
they stood in the temple, "What do you think?
That He will not come to the feast at all?" 57 Now
the chief priests and the Pharisees had given
orders that if anyone knew where He was, he was
to report it, so that they might seize Him.

Mary Anoints Jesus with Costly Perfume

12 Jesus, therefore, six days before the Pass
over, came to Bethany where Lazarus was,
whom Jesus had raised from the dead. 2 So they
made Him a supper there, and Martha was serv-
ing; and Lazarus was one of those reclining *at the*
table with Him. 3 Mary then took a [e]litra of per-
fume of very costly pure nard, and anointed the
feet of Jesus and wiped His feet with her hair; and

e. A Roman pound, approx. 12 oz. or 340 gm

the house was filled with the fragrance of the per-
fume. 4 But Judas Iscariot, one of His disciples, who
was going to betray Him, *said, 5 "Why was this
perfume not sold for three hundred denarii and
given to the poor?" 6 Now he said this, not because
he was concerned about the poor, but because he
was a thief, and as he had the money box, he used
to take from what was put into it. 7 Therefore Jesus
said, "Let her alone, so that she may keep it for the
day of My burial. 8 For you always have the poor
with you, but you do not always have Me."

9 Then the large crowd from the Jews learned
that He was there. And they came, not because of
Jesus only, but that they might also see Lazarus,
whom He raised from the dead. 10 But the chief
priests planned to put Lazarus to death also;
11 because on account of him many of the Jews
were going away and were believing in Jesus.

The Triumphal Entry

12 On the next day the large crowd who had
come to the feast, when they heard that Jesus
was coming to Jerusalem, 13 took the branches of
the palm trees and went out to meet Him, and

began to shout, "Hosanna! BLESSED IS HE WHO COMES IN THE NAME OF THE LORD, even the King of Israel." [14] And Jesus, finding a young donkey, sat on it; as it is written, [15] "FEAR NOT, DAUGHTER OF ZION; BEHOLD, YOUR KING IS COMING, SEATED ON A DONKEY'S COLT." [16] These things His disciples did not understand at the first; but when Jesus was glorified, then they remembered that these things were written about Him, and that they had done these things to Him. [17] So the crowd, who was with Him when He called Lazarus out of the tomb and raised him from the dead, continued to bear witness *about Him.* [18] For this reason also the crowd went and met Him, because they heard that He had done this sign. [19] So the Pharisees said to one another, "You see that you are gaining nothing; look, the world has gone after Him."

Some Greeks Seek Jesus

[20] Now there were some Greeks among those who were going up to worship at the feast; [21] these then came to Philip, who was from Bethsaida of Galilee, and *began to* ask him, saying, "Sir,

we wish to see Jesus." 22 Philip *came and *told
Andrew; Andrew and Philip *came and *told
Jesus. 23 And Jesus *answered them, saying, "The
hour has come for the Son of Man to be glorified.
24 Truly, truly, I say to you, unless a grain of wheat
falls into the earth and dies, it remains alone; but
if it dies, it bears much fruit. 25 He who loves his
life loses it, and he who hates his life in this world
will keep it to life eternal. 26 If anyone serves Me,
he must follow Me; and where I am, there My ser-
vant will be also; if anyone serves Me, the Father
will honor him.

The Son of Man Must Be Lifted Up

27 "Now My soul has become dismayed; and
what shall I say, 'Father, save Me from this hour'?
But for this purpose I came to this hour. 28 Father,
glorify Your name." Then a voice came from
heaven: "I have both glorified it, and will glorify
it again." 29 So the crowd *of people* who stood by
and heard it were saying that it had thundered;
others were saying, "An angel has spoken to
Him." 30 Jesus answered and said, "This voice has
not come for My sake, but for your sake. 31 Now

judgment is upon this world; now the ruler of this
world will be cast out. 32 And I, if I am lifted up
from the earth, will draw all men to Myself." 33 But
He was saying this to indicate the kind of death
by which He was about to die. 34 The crowd then
answered Him, "We have heard from the Law that
the Christ is to remain forever; and how do You
say, 'The Son of Man must be lifted up'? Who is
this Son of Man?" 35 So Jesus said to them, "For a
little while longer the Light is among you. Walk
while you have the Light, so that darkness will
not overtake you; he who walks in the darkness
does not know where he goes. 36 While you have
the Light, believe in the Light, so that you may
become sons of Light."

These things Jesus spoke, and He went away
and hid Himself from them. 37 But though He had
done so many signs before them, they *still* were
not believing in Him, 38 so that the word of Isaiah
the prophet might be fulfilled, which he spoke:
"LORD, WHO HAS BELIEVED OUR REPORT? AND TO
WHOM HAS THE ARM OF THE LORD BEEN REVEALED?"
39 For this reason they could not believe, for Isaiah
said again, 40 "HE HAS BLINDED THEIR EYES AND HE

HARDENED THEIR HEART, LEST THEY SEE WITH THEIR
EYES AND UNDERSTAND WITH THEIR HEART, AND
RETURN AND I HEAL THEM." 41 These things Isaiah
said because he saw His glory, and he spoke about
Him. 42 Nevertheless many even of the rulers
believed in Him, but because of the Pharisees they
were not confessing *Him*, for fear that they would
be put out of the synagogue; 43 for they loved the
glory of men rather than the glory of God.

44 And Jesus cried out and said, "He who
believes in Me, does not believe in Me but in Him
who sent Me. 45 And he who sees Me sees the
One who sent Me. 46 I have come *as* Light into the
world, so that everyone who believes in Me will
not remain in darkness. 47 And if anyone hears
My words and does not keep them, I do not judge
him; for I did not come to judge the world, but
to save the world. 48 He who rejects Me and does
not receive My words, has one who judges him;
the word I spoke is what will judge him on the
last day. 49 For I did not speak from Myself, but
the Father Himself who sent Me has given Me a
commandment—what to say and what to speak.
50 And I know that His commandment is eternal

life; therefore the things I speak, I speak just as
the Father has told Me."

The Lord's Supper

13 Now before the Feast of the Passover,
Jesus knowing that His hour had come that
He would depart out of this world to the Father,
having loved His own who were in the world, He
loved them to the end. 2 And during supper, the
devil having already put into the heart of Judas
Iscariot, *the son* of Simon, to betray Him, 3 *Jesus,*
knowing that the Father had given all things into
His hands, and that He had come forth from God
and was going back to God, 4 *got up from supper,
and *laid aside His garments; and taking a towel,
He tied it around Himself.

Jesus Washes the Disciples' Feet

5 Then He *poured water into the washbasin, and
began to wash the disciples' feet and to wipe them
with the towel which He had tied around *Himself.*
6 So He *came to Simon Peter. He *said to Him,
"Lord, are You going to wash my feet?" 7 Jesus
answered and said to him, "What I am doing you

do not realize now, but you will understand after-
wards." 8 Peter *said to Him, "You will never wash
my feet—ever!" Jesus answered him, "If I do not
wash you, you have no part with Me." 9 Simon
Peter *said to Him, "Lord, not only my feet, but
also my hands and my head." 10 Jesus *said to him,
"He who has bathed needs only to wash his feet,
but is completely clean; and you are clean, but
not all *of you*." 11 For He knew the one who was
betraying Him; for this reason He said, "Not all of
you are clean."

12 So when He had washed their feet, and taken
His garments and reclined *at the table* again, He
said to them, "Do you know what I have done to
you? 13 You call Me Teacher and Lord; and you
are right, for *so* I am. 14 If I then, the Lord and
the Teacher, washed your feet, you also ought to
wash one another's feet. 15 For I gave you an exam-
ple that you also should do as I did to you. 16 Truly,
truly, I say to you, a slave is not greater than his
master, nor *is* one who is sent greater than the
one who sent him. 17 If you know these things, you
are blessed if you do them. 18 I do not speak about
all of you. I know the ones I have chosen; but that

the Scripture may be fulfilled, 'HE WHO EATS MY
BREAD HAS LIFTED UP HIS HEEL AGAINST ME.' 19 From
now on I am telling you before *it* occurs, so that
when it does occur, you may believe that I am *He.*
20 Truly, truly, I say to you, he who receives any-
one I send receives Me; and he who receives Me
receives Him who sent Me."

Jesus Predicts His Betrayal

21 When Jesus had said these things, He became
troubled in spirit, and bore witness and said,
"Truly, truly, I say to you, that one of you will
betray Me." 22 The disciples *began* looking at
one another, perplexed about whom He *spoke.
23 There was reclining on Jesus' bosom one of His
disciples, whom Jesus loved. 24 So Simon Peter
*gestured to him to inquire, "Who is the one of
whom He is speaking?" 25 He, leaning back thus
on Jesus' bosom, *said to Him, "Lord, who is it?"
26 Jesus *answered, "He is the one for whom I shall
dip the piece of bread and give it to him." So when
He had dipped the piece of bread, He *took and
*gave it to Judas, *the son* of Simon Iscariot. 27 And
after the piece of bread, Satan then entered into

him. Therefore Jesus *said to him, "What you do,
do quickly." 28 Now no one of those reclining *at
the table* knew for what purpose He had said this
to him. 29 For some were thinking, because Judas
had the money box, that Jesus was saying to him,
"Buy the things we have need of for the feast"; or
else, that he should give something to the poor.
30 So after receiving the piece of bread, he went out
immediately. And it was night.

31 Therefore when he had gone out, Jesus *said,
"Now is the Son of Man glorified, and God is glo-
rified in Him; 32 if God is glorified in Him, God will
also glorify Him in Himself, and will glorify Him
immediately. 33 Little children, I am with you a lit-
tle while longer. You will seek Me; and as I said to
the Jews, now I also say to you, 'Where I am going,
you cannot come.' 34 A new commandment I give
to you, that you love one another, even as I have
loved you, that you also love one another. 35 By
this all will know that you are My disciples, if you
have love for one another."

36 Simon Peter *said to Him, "Lord, where are
You going?" Jesus answered, "Where I go, you
cannot follow Me now; but you will follow later."

[37] Peter *said to Him, "Lord, why can I not follow
You right now? I will lay down my life for You."
[38] Jesus *answered, "Will you lay down your life
for Me? Truly, truly, I say to you, a rooster will not
crow until you deny Me three times.

I Am the Way, the Truth, and the Life

14 "Do not let your heart be troubled; believe
in God, believe also in Me. [2] In My Father's
house are many dwelling places; if it were not so, I
would have told you; for I go to prepare a place for
you. [3] And if I go and prepare a place for you, I will
come again and receive you to Myself, that where
I am, *there* you may be also. [4] And you know the
way where I am going." [5] Thomas *said to Him,
"Lord, we do not know where You are going. How
do we know the way?" [6] Jesus *said to him, "I am
the way, and the truth, and the life. No one comes
to the Father but through Me.

Oneness with the Father

[7] If you have come to know Me, you will know
My Father also; from now on you know Him, and
have seen Him."

8 Philip *said to Him, "Lord, show us the Father,
and it is enough for us." 9 Jesus *said to him, "Have
I been with you all so long and have you not
come to know Me, Philip? He who has seen Me
has seen the Father; how *can* you say, 'Show us
the Father'? 10 Do you not believe that I am in the
Father, and the Father is in Me? The words that
I say to you I do not speak from Myself, but the
Father abiding in Me does His works. 11 Believe Me
that I am in the Father and the Father is in Me;
otherwise believe because of the works them-
selves. 12 Truly, truly, I say to you, he who believes
in Me, the works that I do, he will do also; and
greater *works* than these he will do because I go
to the Father. 13 Whatever you ask in My name,
this will I do, so that the Father may be glorified
in the Son. 14 If you ask Me anything in My name,
I will do *it*.

15 "If you love Me, you will keep My command-
ments.

Jesus Promises the Holy Spirit

16 And I will ask the Father, and He will give you
another Advocate, that He may be with you

forever; [17] the Spirit of truth, whom the world can-
not receive, because it does not see Him or know
Him. You know Him because He abides with you
and will be in you.

[18] "I will not leave you as orphans; I will come to
you. [19] After a little while the world will no longer
see Me, but you *will* see Me; because I live, you
will live also. [20] On that day you will know that I
am in My Father, and you in Me, and I in you. [21] He
who has My commandments and keeps them is
the one who loves Me; and he who loves Me will
be loved by My Father, and I will love him and will
disclose Myself to him." [22] Judas (not Iscariot) *said
to Him, "Lord, what then has happened that You
are going to disclose Yourself to us and not to the
world?" [23] Jesus answered and said to him, "If any-
one loves Me, he will keep My word; and My Father
will love him, and We will come to him and make
Our dwelling with him. [24] He who does not love Me
does not keep My words; and the word which you
hear is not Mine, but the Father's who sent Me.

[25] "These things I have spoken to you while abid-
ing with you. [26] But the Advocate, the Holy Spirit,
whom the Father will send in My name, He will

teach you all things, and bring to your remem-
brance all that I said to you. 27 Peace I leave with
you; My peace I give to you; not as the world gives
do I give to you. Do not let your heart be troubled,
nor let it be fearful. 28 You heard that I said to you,
'I go away, and I will come to you.' If you loved
Me, you would have rejoiced because I go to the
Father, for the Father is greater than I. 29 And now
I have told you before it happens, so that when
it happens, you may believe. 30 I will not speak
much more with you, for the ruler of the world
is coming, and he has nothing in Me; 31 but so that
the world may know that I love the Father, I do
exactly as the Father commanded Me. Get up, let
us go from here.

I Am the True Vine

15 "I am the true vine, and My Father is the
vine-grower. 2 Every branch in Me that
does not bear fruit, He takes away; and every
branch that bears fruit, He cleans it so that it may
bear more fruit. 3 You are already clean because of
the word which I have spoken to you. 4 Abide in
Me, and I in you. As the branch cannot bear fruit

from itself unless it abides in the vine, so neither
can you unless you abide in Me. [5] I am the vine,
you are the branches; he who abides in Me and
I in him, he bears much fruit, for apart from Me
you can do nothing. [6] If anyone does not abide in
Me, he is thrown away as a branch and dries up;
and they gather them, and cast them into the fire
and they are burned. [7] If you abide in Me, and My
words abide in you, ask whatever you wish, and
it will be done for you. [8] My Father is glorified by
this, that you bear much fruit, and *so* prove to be
My disciples. [9] Just as the Father has loved Me,
I have also loved you; abide in My love. [10] If you
keep My commandments, you will abide in My
love; just as I have kept My Father's commandments and abide in His love. [11] These things I have
spoken to you so that My joy may be in you, and
that your joy may be complete.

Jesus' Commandment Is Love

[12] "This is My commandment, that you love one
another, just as I have loved you. [13] Greater love
has no one than this, that one lay down his life for
his friends. [14] You are My friends if you do what I

command you. [15] No longer do I call you slaves, for
the slave does not know what his master is doing;
but I have called you friends, for all things that I
have heard from My Father I have made known to
you. [16] You did not choose Me but I chose you, and
appointed you that you would go and bear fruit,
and *that* your fruit would abide, so that whatever
you ask of the Father in My name He may give
to you. [17] This I command you, that you love one
another.

If the World Hates You

[18] "If the world hates you, know that it has hated
Me before *it hated* you. [19] If you were of the world,
the world would love its own; but because you are
not of the world, but I chose you out of the world,
because of this the world hates you. [20] Remember
the word that I said to you, 'A slave is not greater
than his master.' If they persecuted Me, they will
also persecute you; if they kept My word, they will
keep yours also. [21] But all these things they will do
to you for My name's sake, because they do not
know the One who sent Me. [22] If I had not come
and spoken to them, they would not have sin, but

now they have no excuse for their sin. 23 He who
hates Me hates My Father also. 24 If I had not done
among them the works which no one else did,
they would not have sin; but now they have both
seen and hated Me and My Father as well. 25 But
this happened to fulfill the word that is written in
their Law, 'THEY HATED ME WITHOUT CAUSE.'
26 "When the Advocate comes, whom I will send
to you from the Father, the Spirit of truth who pro-
ceeds from the Father, He will bear witness about
Me, 27 and you *will* bear witness also, because you
have been with Me from the beginning.

Jesus' Warning

16 "These things I have spoken to you so that
you may be kept from stumbling. 2 They
will put you out of the synagogue, but an hour is
coming for everyone who kills you to think that
he is offering service to God. 3 These things they
will do because they did not know the Father or
Me. 4 But these things I have spoken to you, so that
when their hour comes, you may remember that I
told you of them. These things I did not say to you
at the beginning, because I was with you.

The Spirit Is Promised Again

5 "But now I am going to Him who sent Me; and
none of you asks Me, 'Where are You going?' 6 But
because I have said these things to you, sorrow
has filled your heart. 7 But I tell you the truth, it
is to your advantage that I go away; for if I do not
go away, the Advocate will not come to you; but
if I go, I will send Him to you. 8 And He, when He
comes, will convict the world concerning sin and
righteousness and judgment; 9 concerning sin,
because they do not believe in Me; 10 and concern-
ing righteousness, because I go to the Father and
you no longer see Me; 11 and concerning judgment,
because the ruler of this world has been judged.

12 "I still have many more things to say to you,
but you cannot bear *them* now. 13 But when He,
the Spirit of truth, comes, He will guide you into
all the truth; for He will not speak from Himself,
but whatever He hears, He will speak; and He will
disclose to you what is to come. 14 He will glorify
Me, for He will take of Mine and will disclose *it*
to you. 15 All things that the Father has are Mine;
therefore I said that He takes of Mine and will dis-
close *it* to you.

Sorrow Turned to Joy

16 "A little while, and you will no longer see Me;
and again a little while, and you will see Me."
17 *Some* of His disciples then said to one another,
"What is this He is telling us, 'A little while, and
you will not see Me; and again a little while, and
you will see Me'; and, 'because I go to the Father'?"
18 So they were saying, "What is this that He says,
'A little while'? We do not know what He is talking
about." 19 Jesus knew that they were wishing to
question Him, and He said to them, "Are you
deliberating together about this, that I said, 'A little while, and you will not see Me, and again a little while, and you will see Me'? 20 Truly, truly, I say
to you, that you will cry and lament, but the world
will rejoice; you will be sorrowful, but your sorrow will be turned into joy. 21 Whenever a woman
is in labor she has sorrow, because her hour has
come; but when she gives birth to the child, she
no longer remembers the suffering because of
the joy that a child has been born into the world.
22 Therefore you too have sorrow now; but I will
see you again, and your heart will rejoice, and no
one *will* take your joy away from you.

I Have Overcome the World

23 And on that day you will not question Me about
anything. Truly, truly, I say to you, if you ask the
Father for anything in My name, He will give it to
you. 24 Until now you have asked for nothing in
My name; ask and you will receive, so that your
joy may be made complete.

25 "These things I have spoken to you in figures
of speech; an hour is coming when I will no lon-
ger speak to you in figures of speech, but will tell
you openly of the Father. 26 On that day you will
ask in My name, and I do not say to you that I
will request of the Father on your behalf; 27 for the
Father Himself loves you, because you have loved
Me and have believed that I came forth from the
Father. 28 I came forth from the Father and have
come into the world; I am leaving the world again
and going to the Father."

29 His disciples *said, "Behold, now You are
speaking openly and are not using a figure of
speech. 30 Now we know that You know all things,
and have no need for anyone to question You; by
this we believe that You came from God." 31 Jesus
answered them, "Do you now believe? 32 Behold,

an hour is coming, and has *already* come, for
you to be scattered, each to his own *home*, and to
leave Me alone; and *yet* I am not alone, because
the Father is with Me. 33 These things I have spo-
ken to you, so that in Me you may have peace. In
the world you have tribulation, but take courage;
I have overcome the world."

The High Priestly Prayer

17 Jesus spoke these things; and lifting up His
eyes to heaven, He said, "Father, the hour
has come; glorify Your Son, that the Son may glo-
rify You, 2 even as You gave Him authority over all
flesh, that to all whom You have given Him, He
may give eternal life. 3 And this is eternal life, that
they may know You, the only true God, and Jesus
Christ whom You have sent. 4 I glorified You on the
earth, having finished the work which You have
given Me to do. 5 Now, Father, glorify Me together
with Yourself, with the glory which I had with You
before the world was.

Jesus Prays for His Disciples

6 "I have manifested Your name to the men

whom You gave Me out of the world; they were
Yours and You gave them to Me, and they have
kept Your word. 7 Now they have come to know
that everything You have given Me is from You;
8 for the words which You gave Me I have given to
them; and they received *them* and truly under-
stood that I came forth from You, and they
believed that You sent Me. 9 I ask on their behalf;
I do not ask on behalf of the world but of those
whom You have given Me; for they are Yours;
10 and all things that are Mine are Yours, and Yours
are Mine; and I have been glorified in them. 11 And
I am no longer in the world; and *yet* they them-
selves are in the world, and I come to You. Holy
Father, keep them in Your name, *the name* which
You have given Me, that they may be one even as
We *are*. 12 While I was with them, I was keeping
them in Your name which You have given Me; and
I guarded them and not one of them perished but
the son of perdition, so that the Scripture would
be fulfilled. 13 But now I come to You; and these
things I speak in the world so that they may have
My joy made full in themselves. 14 I have given
them Your word; and the world has hated them,

because they are not of the world, even as I am
not of the world. [15] I do not ask You to take them
out of the world, but to keep them from the evil
one. [16] They are not of the world, even as I am not
of the world. [17] Sanctify them by the truth; Your
word is truth. [18] As You sent Me into the world, I
also sent them into the world. [19] For their sake I
sanctify Myself, that they themselves also may be
sanctified in truth.

[20] "I do not ask on behalf of these alone, but for
those also who believe in Me through their word;
[21] that they may all be one; even as You, Father,
are in Me and I in You, that they also may be in
Us, so that the world may believe that You sent
Me. [22] The glory which You have given Me I have
given to them, that they may be one, just as We
are one; [23] I in them and You in Me, that they may
be perfected in unity, so that the world may know
that You sent Me, and loved them, even as You
have loved Me. [24] Father, I desire that they also,
whom You have given Me, be with Me where I am,
so that they may see My glory which You have
given Me, for You loved Me before the foundation
of the world.

25 "O righteous Father, although the world has
not known You, yet I have known You; and these
have known that You sent Me; 26 and I have made
Your name known to them, and will make it
known, so that the love with which You loved Me
may be in them, and I in them."

Jesus Betrayed and Arrested

18 When Jesus had spoken these words, He
went forth with His disciples to the other
side of the Kidron Valley, where there was a gar-
den, into which He entered with His disciples.
2 Now Judas also, who was betraying Him, knew
the place, for Jesus had often gathered there with
His disciples. 3 Judas then, having received the
Roman cohort and officers from the chief priests
and the Pharisees, *came there with lanterns and
torches and weapons. 4 So Jesus, knowing all the
things that were coming upon Him, went forth
and *said to them, "Whom do you seek?" 5 They
answered Him, "Jesus the Nazarene." He *said to
them, "I am *He*." And Judas also, who was betray-
ing Him, was standing with them. 6 So when He
said to them, "I am *He*," they drew back and fell

to the ground. 7 Therefore He again asked them,
"Whom do you seek?" And they said, "Jesus the
Nazarene." 8 Jesus answered, "I told you that I am
He; so if you seek Me, let these go their way," 9 in
order that the word which He spoke would be ful-
filled, "Of those whom You have given Me, I lost
not one." 10 Simon Peter then, having a sword,
drew it and struck the high priest's slave, and
cut off his right ear; and the slave's name was
Malchus. 11 So Jesus said to Peter, "Put the sword
into the sheath; the cup which the Father has
given Me, shall I not drink it?"

Jesus Before the Priests; Peter Denies Jesus

12 So the *Roman* cohort and the commander and
the officers of the Jews, arrested Jesus and bound
Him, 13 and led Him to Annas first; for he was
father-in-law of Caiaphas, who was high priest
that year. 14 Now Caiaphas was the one who had
advised the Jews that it was better for one man to
die on behalf of the people.

15 And Simon Peter was following Jesus, and
so was another disciple. Now that disciple was
known to the high priest, and entered with Jesus

into the court of the high priest, [16] but Peter was
standing at the door outside. So the other disci-
ple, who was known to the high priest, went out
and spoke to the doorkeeper, and brought Peter
in. [17] Then the servant-girl who kept the door *said
to Peter, "Are you not also *one* of this man's disci-
ples?" He *said, "I am not." [18] Now the slaves and
the officers were standing *there*, having made a
charcoal fire, for it was cold and they were warm-
ing themselves; and Peter was also with them,
standing and warming himself.

[19] The high priest then questioned Jesus about
His disciples, and about His teaching. [20] Jesus
answered him, "I have spoken openly to the
world; I always taught in synagogues and in the
temple, where all the Jews come together; and I
spoke nothing in secret. [21] Why do you question
Me? Question those who have heard what I spoke
to them; behold, they know what I said." [22] And
when He had said this, one of the officers stand-
ing nearby gave Jesus a slap, saying, "Is that the
way You answer the high priest?" [23] Jesus answered
him, "If I have spoken wrongly, bear witness of
the wrong; but if rightly, why do you strike Me?"

24 So Annas sent Him bound to Caiaphas the high
priest.
25 Now Simon Peter was standing and warming
himself. So they said to him, "You are not also *one*
of His disciples, are you?" He denied *it*, and said,
"I am not." 26 One of the slaves of the high priest,
being a relative of the one whose ear Peter cut off,
*said, "Did I not see you in the garden with Him?"
27 Peter then denied *it* again, and immediately a
rooster crowed.

Jesus Before Pilate

28 Then they *led Jesus from Caiaphas into the
Praetorium, and it was early; and they them-
selves did not enter into the Praetorium so that
they would not be defiled, but might eat the
Passover. 29 Therefore Pilate went out to them
and *said, "What accusation do you bring against
this man?" 30 They answered and said to him, "If
this man were not an evildoer, we would not have
delivered Him to you." 31 So Pilate said to them,
"Take Him yourselves, and judge Him accord-
ing to your law." The Jews said to him, "It is not
lawful for us to put anyone to death," 32 in order

that the word of Jesus which He spoke would be
fulfilled, signifying by what kind of death He was
about to die.

33 Therefore Pilate entered again into the
Praetorium, and summoned Jesus and said to
Him, "Are You the King of the Jews?" 34 Jesus
answered, "Are you saying this from yourself, or
did others tell you about Me?" 35 Pilate answered,
"Am I a Jew? Your own nation and the chief priests
delivered You to me; what did You do?" 36 Jesus
answered, "My kingdom is not of this world. If
My kingdom were of this world, then My servants
would be fighting so that I would not be delivered
over to the Jews; but as it is, My kingdom is not
from here." 37 Therefore Pilate said to Him, "So
You are a king?" Jesus answered, "You yourself
said I am a king. For this I have been born, and for
this I have come into the world, to bear witness to
the truth. Everyone who is of the truth hears My
voice." 38 Pilate *said to Him, "What is truth?"

And when he had said this, he went out again
to the Jews and *said to them, "I find no guilt in
Him. 39 But you have a custom that I release some-
one for you at the Passover; do you wish then

that I release for you the King of the Jews?" 40 So
they cried out again, saying, "Not this man, but
Barabbas." Now Barabbas was a robber.

Jesus Flogged and Rejected as King

19 Pilate then took Jesus and flogged Him.
2 And when the soldiers twisted together
a crown of thorns, they put it on His head, and
put a purple robe on Him; 3 and they were com-
ing to Him and saying, "Hail, King of the Jews!"
and were giving Him slaps *in the face.* 4 And Pilate
came out again and *said to them, "Behold, I am
bringing Him out to you so that you may know
that I find no guilt in Him." 5 Jesus then came out,
wearing the crown of thorns and the purple robe.
Pilate *said to them, "Behold, the man!" 6 So when
the chief priests and the officers saw Him, they
cried out saying, "Crucify, crucify!" Pilate *said
to them, "Take Him yourselves and crucify Him,
for I find no guilt in Him." 7 The Jews answered
him, "We have a law, and by that law He ought to
die because He made Himself out *to be* the Son
of God."

8 Therefore when Pilate heard this statement,

he became more afraid; 9 and he entered into the
Praetorium again and *said to Jesus, "Where are
You from?" But Jesus gave him no answer. 10 So
Pilate *said to Him, "You do not speak to me?
Do You not know that I have authority to release
You, and I have authority to crucify You?" 11 Jesus
answered, "You would have no authority over
Me, unless it had been given you from above; for
this reason he who delivered Me to you has *the*
greater sin." 12 As a result of this Pilate kept seek-
ing to release Him, but the Jews cried out saying,
"If you release this man, you are no friend of
Caesar; everyone who makes himself *to be* a king
opposes Caesar."

13 Therefore when Pilate heard these words,
he brought Jesus out, and sat down on the judg-
ment seat at a place called The Stone Pavement,
but in Hebrew, Gabbatha. 14 Now it was the day
of Preparation for the Passover; it was about the
sixth hour. And he *said to the Jews, "Behold, your
King!" 15 So they cried out, "Away with *Him*! Away
with *Him*! Crucify Him!" Pilate *said to them,
"Shall I crucify your King?" The chief priests
answered, "We have no king but Caesar."

The Crucifixion

16 So he then delivered Him over to them to be
crucified.
17 They took Jesus, therefore, and He went
out, bearing His own cross, to the place called
the Place of a Skull, which is called in Hebrew,
Golgotha. 18 There they crucified Him, and with
Him two other men, one on either side, and Jesus
in between. 19 And Pilate also wrote an inscription
and put it on the cross. It was written, "JESUS
THE NAZARENE, THE KING OF THE JEWS."
20 Therefore many of the Jews read this inscrip-
tion, for the place where Jesus was crucified was
near the city; and it was written in Hebrew, Latin,
and in Greek. 21 So the chief priests of the Jews
were saying to Pilate, "Do not write, 'The King
of the Jews;' but that He said, 'I am King of the
Jews.' " 22 Pilate answered, "What I have written I
have written."
23 Then the soldiers, when they had crucified
Jesus, took His garments and made four parts, a
part to each soldier and *also* His tunic; now that
tunic was seamless, woven in one piece from the
top. 24 So they said to one another, "Let us not

tear it, but cast lots for it, *to decide* whose it shall
be;" *this was* in order that the Scripture would
be fulfilled: "THEY DIVIDED MY GARMENTS AMONG
THEM, AND FOR MY CLOTHING THEY CAST LOTS."
25 Therefore the soldiers did these things.
But standing by the cross of Jesus were His
mother, and His mother's sister, Mary the *wife*
of Clopas, and Mary Magdalene. 26 When Jesus
then saw His mother, and the disciple whom He
loved standing nearby, He *said to His mother,
"Woman, behold, your son!" 27 Then He *said to
the disciple, "Behold, your mother!" From that
hour the disciple took her into his *home*.

Scripture Fulfilled—It Is Finished

28 After this, Jesus, knowing that all things
had already been finished, in order to finish the
Scripture, *said, "I am thirsty." 29 A jar full of sour
wine was standing there; so they put a sponge
full of the sour wine upon *a branch of* hyssop
and brought it up to His mouth. 30 Therefore
when Jesus had received the sour wine, He said,
"It is finished!" And bowing His head, He gave up
His spirit.

31 Then the Jews, because it was the day of
Preparation, so that the bodies would not remain
on the cross on the Sabbath (for that Sabbath was
a high day), asked Pilate that their legs might be
broken, and *that* they might be taken away. 32 So
the soldiers came, and broke the legs of the first
man and of the other who was crucified with Him;
33 but coming to Jesus, when they saw that He was
already dead, they did not break His legs. 34 But one
of the soldiers pierced His side with a spear, and
immediately blood and water came out. 35 And he
who has seen has borne witness, and his witness
is true; and he knows that he is telling the truth,
so that you also may believe. 36 For these things
came to pass in order that the Scripture would be
fulfilled, "NOT A BONE OF HIM SHALL BE BROKEN."
37 And again another Scripture says, "THEY SHALL
LOOK ON HIM WHOM THEY PIERCED."

Jesus Is Buried

38 Now after these things Joseph of Arimathea,
being a disciple of Jesus, but secretly because of
his fear of the Jews, asked Pilate that he might
take away the body of Jesus; and Pilate granted

permission. So he came and took away His body.
39 And Nicodemus, who had first come to Him by
night, also came, bringing a mixture of myrrh and
aloes, *weighing* about one hundred litras. 40 So they
took the body of Jesus and bound it in linen wrap-
pings with the spices, as is the burial custom of the
Jews. 41 Now in the place where He was crucified
there was a garden, and in the garden a new tomb
in which no one had yet been laid. 42 Therefore
because of the Jewish day of Preparation, since the
tomb was nearby, they laid Jesus there.

The Empty Tomb

20 Now on the first *day* of the week, Mary
Magdalene *came early to the tomb, while
it *was still dark, and *saw the stone *already* taken
away from the tomb. 2 So she *ran and *came to
Simon Peter and to the other disciple whom Jesus
loved, and *said to them, "They have taken away
the Lord out of the tomb, and we do not know
where they have laid Him." 3 So Peter and the other
disciple went forth, and they were going to the
tomb. 4 And the two were running together; and
the other disciple ran ahead faster than Peter and

came to the tomb first; 5 and stooping and looking
in, he *saw the linen wrappings lying *there*; but he
did not go in. 6 And so Simon Peter also *came, fol-
lowing him, and entered the tomb; and he *saw the
linen wrappings lying there, 7 and the face-cloth
which had been on His head, not lying with the
linen wrappings, but folded up in a place by itself.
8 So the other disciple who had first come to the
tomb then also entered, and he saw and believed.
9 For as yet they did not understand the Scripture,
that He must rise again from the dead. 10 So the dis-
ciples went away again to where they were staying.

Jesus Appears to Mary Magdalene

11 But Mary was standing outside the tomb cry-
ing; and so, as she was crying, she stooped to look
into the tomb; 12 and she *saw two angels in white
sitting, one at the head and one at the feet, where
the body of Jesus had been lying. 13 And they *said
to her, "Woman, why are you crying?" She *said
to them, "Because they have taken away my Lord,
and I do not know where they have laid Him."
14 When she had said this, she turned around and
*saw Jesus standing *there*, and did not know that

it was Jesus. 15 Jesus *said to her, "Woman, why are
you crying? Whom are you seeking?" Thinking
Him to be the gardener, she *said to Him, "Sir,
if you have carried Him away, tell me where you
have laid Him, and I will take Him away." 16 Jesus
*said to her, "Mary!" She turned and *said to Him
in Hebrew, "Rabboni!" (which means, Teacher).
17 Jesus *said to her, "Stop clinging to Me, for I
have not yet ascended to the Father; but go to My
brothers and say to them, 'I ascend to My Father
and your Father, and My God and your God.' "
18 Mary Magdalene *came, announcing to the dis-
ciples, "I have seen the Lord," and *that* He had
said these things to her.

Jesus Appears to His Disciples

19 So while it was evening on that day, the first
day of the week, and while the doors were shut
where the disciples were, for fear of the Jews,
Jesus came and stood in their midst and *said to
them, "Peace *be* with you." 20 And when He had
said this, He showed them both His hands and
His side. The disciples then rejoiced when they
saw the Lord. 21 So Jesus said to them again, "Peace

be with you; as the Father has sent Me, I also send
you." 22 And when He had said this, He breathed
on *them* and *said to them, "Receive the Holy
Spirit. 23 If you forgive the sins of any, *their sins*
have been forgiven them; if you retain the *sins* of
any, they have been retained."
24 But Thomas, one of the twelve, called
Didymus, was not with them when Jesus came.
25 So the other disciples were saying to him, "We
have seen the Lord!" But he said to them, "Unless
I see in His hands the imprint of the nails, and put
my finger into the place of the nails, and put my
hand into His side, I will not believe."
26 And after eight days His disciples were again
inside, and Thomas with them. Jesus *came, the
doors having been shut, and stood in their midst
and said, "Peace *be* with you." 27 Then He *said
to Thomas, "Bring your finger here, and see My
hands; and bring your hand *here* and put it into
My side; and do not be unbelieving, but believ-
ing." 28 Thomas answered and said to Him, "My
Lord and my God!" 29 Jesus *said to him, "Because
you have seen Me, have you believed? Blessed *are*
those who did not see, and *yet* believed."

Why This Gospel Was Written

30 Therefore many other signs Jesus also did in
the presence of the disciples, which are not writ-
ten in this book; 31 but these have been written so
that you may believe that Jesus is the Christ, the
Son of God; and that believing you may have life
in His name.

Jesus Appears at the Sea of Galilee

21 After these things Jesus manifested Himself
again to the disciples at the Sea of Tiberias,
and He manifested *Himself* in this way. 2 Simon
Peter, and Thomas called Didymus, and Nathanael
of Cana in Galilee, and the *sons* of Zebedee, and
two others of His disciples were together. 3 Simon
Peter *said to them, "I am going fishing." They
*said to him, "We will also come with you." They
went out and got into the boat; and that night
they caught nothing.

4 But when the day was now breaking, Jesus
stood on the beach; yet the disciples did not
know that it was Jesus. 5 So Jesus *said to them,
"Children, do you have any fish?" They answered
Him, "No." 6 And He said to them, "Cast the net on

the right side of the boat and you will find *some*."
So they cast, and then they were not able to haul it
in because of the great number of fish. 7 Therefore
that disciple whom Jesus loved *said to Peter, "It is
the Lord." So when Simon Peter heard that it was
the Lord, he put his outer garment on (for he was
stripped *for work*), and cast himself into the sea.
8 But the other disciples came in the little boat, for
they were not far from the land, but about [f]two
hundred cubits away, dragging the net *full* of fish.

9 So when they got out on the land, they *saw
a charcoal fire in place and fish placed on it, and
bread. 10 Jesus *said to them, "Bring some of the
fish which you have now caught." 11 Simon Peter
went up and drew the net to land, full of large
fish, 153; and although there were so many, the
net was not torn.

Jesus Provides Breakfast

12 Jesus *said to them, "Come, have breakfast."
None of the disciples dared to question Him,
"Who are You?" knowing that it was the Lord.
13 Jesus *came and *took the bread and *gave *it* to

---

f. Approx. 98 yds. or 91 m, a cubit was approx. 18 in. or 45 cm

them, and the fish likewise. [14] This is now the third time that Jesus was manifested to the disciples, after He was raised from the dead.

Peter's Restoration and Commission

[15] So when they had finished breakfast, Jesus *said to Simon Peter, "Simon, *son* of John, do you love Me more than these?" He *said to Him, "Yes, Lord; You know that I love You." He *said to him, "Tend My lambs." [16] He *said to him again a second time, "Simon, *son* of John, do you love Me?" He *said to Him, "Yes, Lord; You know that I love You." He *said to him, "Shepherd My sheep." [17] He *said to him the third time, "Simon, *son* of John, do you love Me?" Peter was grieved because He said to him the third time, "Do you love Me?" And he said to Him, "Lord, You know all things; You know that I love You." Jesus *said to him, "Tend My sheep. [18] Truly, truly, I say to you, when you were younger, you used to gird yourself and walk wherever you wished; but when you grow old, you will stretch out your hands and someone else will gird you, and bring you where you do not wish to *go*." [19] Now this He said, signifying by what kind

of death he would glorify God. And when He had
spoken this, He *said to him, "Follow Me!"

Jesus' Command to Follow Him

20 Peter, turning around, *saw the disciple whom
Jesus loved following *them*; the one who also had
leaned back on His bosom at the supper and said,
"Lord, who is the one who betrays You?" 21 So Peter
seeing him *said to Jesus, "Lord, and what about
this man?" 22 Jesus *said to him, "If I want him to
remain until I come, what *is that* to you? You fol-
low Me!" 23 Therefore this saying went out among
the brothers that this disciple would not die; yet
Jesus did not say to him that he would not die, but
only, "If I want him to remain until I come, what
is that to you?"

24 This is the disciple who is bearing witness to
these things and wrote these things, and we know
that his witness is true.

25 And there are also many other things which
Jesus did, which if they *were written one after the
other, I suppose that even the world itself *could
not contain the books that *would be written.

50 Years of Translation History, Continued

LEGACY
STANDARD
BIBLE

"It is the best English translation I have ever read!"

- John MacArthur -